To my love.
Forever yours.

x Ana x

How many of us hold to our hearts the
dream of loving and being loved?

Here is that dream portrayed in verse.
Discover the great unfolding love story;
the inspirational roots being planted in
destiny and distance.

~May Life thrive as an ultimate expression of
Love and may Love return that honour~

love should be *Bountiful*

Life Defined.

What choice have we, within our life defined?
Do we choose love, or on our path does us it find?
  Our world gives birth to every counted soul,
Then nurtures our incentive to reach our charted
                                        goal.

  Then what of life, that raises us expectantly
  To tear emotions as the pounding of the sea;
    That holds us close, as if in arms so sure,
Then tosses us in life, that we must swim to shore.
  What does it teach, what is it all about,
  That we must learn to laugh, to cry, to shout?
  That we, in part, must grow in all these things
  And only when it's done, will we know love,
                              find wings.

  Life's not for us, in whole, to choose our way
  Though we, in part, find words and have a say.
  It is the other strength that bends our journey so,
    Directing us in love, to stand or go.
  It is the inner strength, that when the battles
                                rage
  Guides the written hand upon life's empty page;
  That helps us write new words, a chapter yet
                                unread,
  So on the unmarked road, always we are led.

Love Lasting

It's been so long since you first held me
In your arms and stole that kiss.
More than years since you first told me
How you felt, oh heavenly bliss:
We've travelled far upon our journey
Taken side roads here and there
Pulled apart and drawn together,
Stood alone and as a pair.

It's been so long since you first took me
To the zoo in early Spring;
Since we promised, so sincerely
Committed love, to each we'd bring.
Though our love was sorely tested
In the Winter of romance,
Through it bloomed the rose of Summer,
Growing strong and straight in stance.

It's been so long since you first met me,
Wrote our names upon a wall,
Yet, my love you stand beside me,
Now it seems no time at all.
We will catch a thought, in dreaming,
Memorize the times we've spent:
Knowing true love lasts forever,
Knowing you and I were meant.

love should be **Patient**

Memory's Store.

I sat in my garden this afternoon,
  My heart and my life were quite in tune.
My mind was at peace, the breeze it was kind,
  It wafted you gently through my mind,
Thoughts were soon flooding from memory's
                   store.
And when they subsided I searched for more
To bring you much closer, though not by my side
On wings of my daydreams, to you I can ride.
  You fill my fancies, you touch my heart
    Never now parted, though often apart.
I can pull jewels from star-spangled nights
Diamonds from tear-drops caught in the light.
  Velvet of cuddles, tender, sincere
  Chasing the cobwebs of irrational fear.
  Tender these moments when memories voice
The joy of our laughter, the gift of free choice.
  Dancing at parties, or moving as one,
Sharing sea-spangles that shine in the sun.
  Water and waiting, boats at low tide,
  More to discover, though nothing to hide.
  The afternoon's resting by evening's door,
It's time now to close old memory's store;
But I'll hold one to me, golden and true,
  It's the one where you whispered,
    "I Love You, too."

love should be

Affectio

*etan

Destiny

What brought us together, what pulled us apart,
Was it controlled by the strings of the heart?
  The first formal meeting; professional stance;
Drawn like magnets; the laugh and the glance,
  Then the warm handshake and a soft smile
Soon we were walking the first lovers mile.
Was it by chance that we'd met that day,
  Had destiny found it's own part to play?
Strange how familiar the face and the look,
Like seeing the play, having first read the book,
  Some say that life is a day to day choice,
  Others, that fate must too have a voice.
  I know not the answer though firmly believe
    Destiny bids when to enter and leave
The stage of our life span, the scene and the set,
That's why I know 't was fate that we met.
Fate brought us together and pulled us apart,
Though always controlled by the strings of
              the heart.

love should be Nurturing

The Daisies Were Asleep

The daisies were asleep when I awoke,
My garden lay so silent, no blackbird spoke.
No cawing crows or jackdaws, noisy crowd,
No drop of rain from early morning cloud.
Still asleep the worms beneath the earth,
The chorus of the birds left unrehearsed.
It seems that only I awoke the day:
Should I phone you, what should I say?

I took a china mug from off the rack
And sugar, spoon and tea, then put them back.
I did not need to hear a noisy kettle boil,
But from my kitchen window watch silent stems uncoil.
I gently hugged myself, the room was cool,
Too early for the sun, should it come out at all.
Yet in the early light that touched the trees
I felt it could be you, you touching me.

The daisies were asleep when I awoke,
But turned in universal face as morning broke.
A blackbird called...the worms churned on
And from a budding tree, a robin's song.
So from the east, the palest light of sun
Gave colour to the day, new day begun.
As I watched I knew that I was not alone;
I dialled a chosen number...and you picked up
your phone.

love should be

Dedicated

Love Light

Has there ever been a love as this
That brings such joy in a simple kiss?
That climbs such heights upon a touch,
And whispers in each sweet caress,
"I love you much."
Never on this earth has such a love been made,
That brightens in the light and does not fade
And never will our love die as a day
But light nocturnal dark to show the way.
Always will my heart beat in time with yours,
Bringing both contentment and our lives
new cause.

love should be Loyal

Strength in Truth

I stand before you, naked, unashamed,
Not just my cloak I wear, of tactile skin
But spirit brave though vulnerably exposed,
Yet of great strength from deep within.

♥

I bare my soul to every question you may ask
In hope in searching, answers we may find.
But in your asking treat me well
For my loving spirit needs you to be kind.

♥

I give my heart, examine at your will,
It lies at last within your open palm.
Look well and see this creature beat and bleed,
Yet peaceful now - it knows you mean no harm.

♥

Nothing now is hidden - strength and weakness both.
I rise before you gladly, my passion true.
Judge me not too harshly - as I have judged myself
Then when the time is ready, let me come to you.

♥

All the questions asked, I have asked myself
Yet my feet of clay were not self made.
The canvas of a life well walked upon and trod
Must hold a thread or two that's frayed.

♥

Take me now complete - in the knowledge that my heart
With virgin blood, beats true.
Let me stand before you, naked in the light
And let the God in me, shine for you.

Love should be Sincere

A Special Love

No one could share a kiss the way we do,
    Nor be worthy of such love, a love so true.
No touch could feed the fire with such intent,
    Nor bodies lie so peaceful, in deep content;
    And none will ever know such joy of heart.
Together in our sharing, together when apart.
    Few will ever witness such love not born of man,
    Woven with a destiny of spirits earthly plan.

LYNN NEW ©

love should be Natural

Departure

The image that I hold is in my mind
On quiet days, in simple ways, his face I find.
So clear in every way that picture I recall.
So hard and painful is the fact, he is not here at all.

I recall his face, his pale brow
And when I am alone I will remember how
We said our last goodbyes and held so tight
Fearing love may die when out of sight.

I cannot forget that Summer rain
The moisture on his cheek that emphasised the pain.
Nor our reaching hands, or last caress.
Would the cause of parting make him love me less?

Oh, the wretched train-like resting snake,
Poised to make the journey I am bound to take.
The carriage window open, we reach to reassure
Midst the throbbing diesel and the slamming door.

I recall the touch of fingertips
The blow of kisses sent from trembling lips.
The wave of hand ... oh cruel fate
For any words of love fall now too late.

I remember him diminishing in size.
The last coach obscured him, rain then blurred my eyes.
Yet I recall a stillness in my aching heart
For we would learn of loving while we were apart.

love should be Loving

▸ The Trans-Canadian Train ▸

Oh silver snake, let me acknowledge you for what
you are.
No ordinary train that travels long & travels far,
But one that answers prayers & carries dreamers
such as I
who want to breathe The Rockies air & touch the
prairie sky.

Oh silver snake that carries me to mirrored lakes,
tree lined,
That climbs from valley floor in gentle wind
And takes me to a world where strong free eagles
soar,
Where nature lives its life and makes the law.

Oh silver snake that throbs with life, own life on board
You took a steadfast aim not to be ignored.
Straight arrows route from blasted mountain's core
That took the lives of working men, by the living score.

Oh silver snake, I thank them from my heart.
It was a dream of mine, just once to be a part;
With you I journey westward, coast to coast.
Of Canada's experience, I make the most.

For silver snake, no other name will do,
You wend your way & find me yet another distant view.
Soon I'll return to England, a new life there to claim
But I shall hold the memory of...
The Trans-Canadian train!

LYNN NEW ©

love should be Demonstra *evita

Natural Spirit

Open your hand with the palm held upward
So the deer may openly feed
For the love that you hold, it must be told
He will follow, though often he'll lead.

Hold out your hand with your fingers outstretching
Reach, so the deer will learn trust.
Be steady and firm and soon he will learn
That your heart is of truth and is just.

Give now your hand, in a gesture of welcome
Beckon the animal near.
Be quiet, be still, you mean it no ill
Fear not and he will not fear.

Now hold in your hand your heart for the
giving,
But open, the deer of life senses.
He too has a voice, a freedom of choice
So capture with love, not with fences.

Why?

Why am I not beside you
At the closing of the night,
As the dawn light strengthens
And the curtains fracture light?
Why am I not still with you
As you deeply sleep?
For I still hear you breathing
Rhythmical and deep.
My love, I still can feel you
Warm beneath my touch,
In your sleep be with me
For I love you much.
I pretend that I am kissing
Your face and sleeping eyes
And though we're not together
To you my dear heart flies.
So in your gentle slumber
At the dawning of this day
Know my heart lies with you
And there my love will stay.

Spirit Dwelling

Flying freedom in my heart
Pulls me close towards you, though apart.
Catch and hold it to you, I will appear
Feel the gentle breeze upon your ear.

Longing makes the journey home
Though my body takes me ere to roam.
See the rippled water as the currents run
And as it laps the shoreline, so we touch as one.

Loving lies with you at night
That when you sleep, the moon will light
A tender warmth when resting on your cheek;
It will be me, 'tis you I seek.

Wanting wakes the sleepy day,
Close beside you will my spirit stay
And follow you till you again may rest
Your tired head against the pillow of my breast.

Distant dreams become reality,
I will return, flesh covered spirit will you see
And yet in truth we've spent no time apart
For each of us has dwelt within the other's beating
heart.

LYNN NEW ©

love should be Trusting

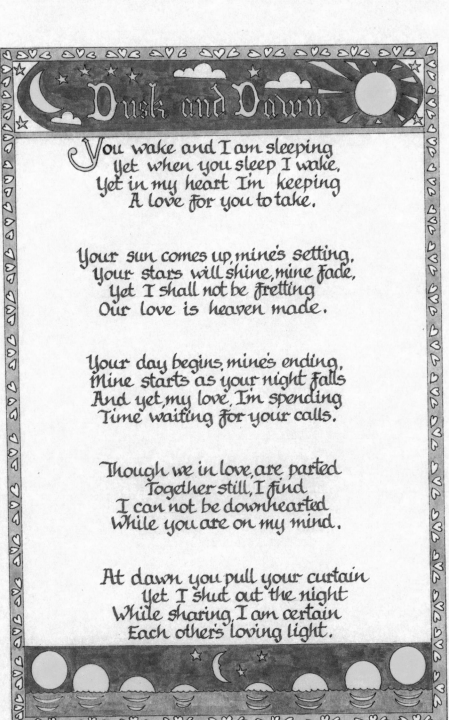

Dusk and Dawn

You wake and I am sleeping
  Yet when you sleep I wake.
Yet in my heart I'm keeping
  A love for you to take.

Your sun comes up, mine's setting,
  Your stars will shine, mine fade.
  Yet I shall not be fretting
Our love is heaven made.

Your day begins, mine's ending,
  Mine starts as your night falls
And yet, my love, I'm spending
  Time waiting for your calls.

Though we in love, are parted
  Together still, I find
I can not be downhearted
While you are on my mind.

At dawn you pull your curtain
  Yet I shut out the night
While sharing, I am certain
  Each other's loving light.

love should be

Appreci

evita

Rockies Call

Day breaks, the mountains call
But not these, I see, not these at all.
Sun starts her journey through the sky,
Between concrete towers rising by and by.
Birds call in chorus, imagination's grand,
For I still hear the Master's voice from another land.
Yet as I look through my restricted view
Still I see the mountains 'gainst the early blue
And somewhere in my heart all nature does respond
To my call of longing, from the land of which I'm fond,
For the Master's mountains and the river's icy flow,
For the smell of larch and pine and the raven's crow.
Oh city as you early stir, yet never seeming sleep
Take not from me the memory, so my dreams I'll keep.
Let my heart, this early day, feel an inner swell
For the land I've left behind, where elk and eagles dwell.
And as my thoughts spin upward from the city's stirring drone,
Let me carry in my heart, the Rockies dream I've known.

The Arrival.

Will he be waiting, oh does he care?
Will he be waiting, oh will he be there?
My train rattles onward, my journey too slow.
Will he be waiting? I really don't know.

Will he step forward, with love in his heart
To pick up my case so we can depart?
My journey's frustrating, I'm tired and ill fed.
Will he still love me? Such thoughts fill my head.

Will he still love me, or has his mood changed?
Will he be waiting as we had arranged?
My train rattles onward, too slowly for me,
But surely it takes me to where I must be.

We stop at the stations, or slow on the track.
Doesn't the engine know I must be back?
How will he look; what will he wear?
Oh hurry train, I have to be there!

Just as I think, this torture won't end,
We pass the last signal and turn the last bend.
I'm sick with excitement and weak at the knees.
Will he even like me? Will my face please?

The motion has halted, my journey complete;
I look for the face of the man I shall meet.
Will he still love me, will he still care?
Oh, I can not see him; ah yes, he is there!

The birds in my heart burst through my chest.
Our love through our parting has stood a fair test.
His hand carries roses, his face wears a smile
That tells me he loves me and has, all the while.

Now as I get closer, he starts to unroll
Hand written wording on a white scroll.
He holds it up bravely for the world now to see
The red written letters "Will you marry me?"

love should be Respectful

Complete Love

Love is many things
To laugh and cry.
To reach the heavens with great joy
Or fall and wish to die.

Love is for the living,
Whole, complete,
Fearful of the parting
Excitement when we meet.

Love is for the longing,
The dream to touch.
Fearful of rejection.
Can we love too much?

Love is in the asking
For time to heal and lie
In each others arms,
A time to cry.

Love is felt in sharing
The spirit of our love
With the One who guides us
Patiently above.

love should be Sentimental

The Struggling Rose

Everything is rosy
Behind the garden wall.
That is what they always think
Though it's not true at all.
Life is always easy
That's what they make out.
Quick to show their envy
But really they know nought.
There is always someone
Who thinks he knows it all.
Spreading verbal poison
Hoping others fall.
I suppose it's human instinct
A trait of jealous pride
But no-one knows another's truth
It's something we all hide.
There's no way of knowing
That, behind the garden wall
There's weeds amongst the roses
Growing just as tall
And the owner of the garden
Must work with torn hands
Till the weeds are vanquished
And the rose in glory stands.
Folk will whisper ignorance
That others loudly hear,
But who will tell the listener,
"Things aren't as they appear"?
So he who works behind the wall
Must contented be
That those who spread their gossip
His rose they'll never see.

LYNN NEW ©

love should be...

Adoring

What Use?

What use is love
　　Without the pain of longing,
The thought of home
　　Without belonging?
What is a joy
　　Without a kiss to share,
A hug or touch
　　To show you care?
What is love
　　Without the swift emotion?
No more than shore
　　Without the storm-whipped ocean.
What good is light
　　Without the contrast of the shade,
Or flower bed
　　Without the rose God made?
What use my voice
　　If I can't call your name
That you would hear
　　And answer me the same?
What use the years
　　Or moments till I die,
Without your love
　　What use am I?

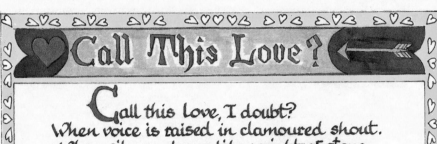

Call This Love?

Call this love, I doubt?
When voice is raised in clamoured shout.
When silence drops like weight of stone;
From love's great heights to depths we're thrown.

Call this love? The bed lies cold.
No-one to clasp, no face to hold.
The turning from and sleeping stiff,
Will love return from lovers' tiff?

Call this love? No sharing thought,
Nor secret glance that love has taught.
No lips to kiss, a slight turned cheek.
No words to hear and few to speak.

Call this love? I doubt it not,
From Cupid's bow the arrows shot
To find its mark, thrust very deep
With tears of pain and joy to weep.

Call this love? No other name
Can tear emotions quite the same;
But when it hurts and loves amiss
Part not but seal it with a kiss.

love should be Inspiring

Whispers • Laughter • Secrets • Shouts

Nicknames

Pigswine and Plonker
What's in a name?
Something to call
When love is a game.
A word of endearment,
A secret between
A man and a woman
And what it may mean.
Worth more than a cuddle
When words have been fraught,
Defusing the tension
With humour, of sort.
It hints of an intimate
Knowledge you share
With the partner you love
And for whom you care.
Perhaps to be shouted
Or whispered quite low
The meaning is only
For you both to know.
The names you are born with
Are ones others call
But for Pigswine and Plonker
These names say it all!

Secret Meanings

LYNN NEW ©

love should be non-conform animo

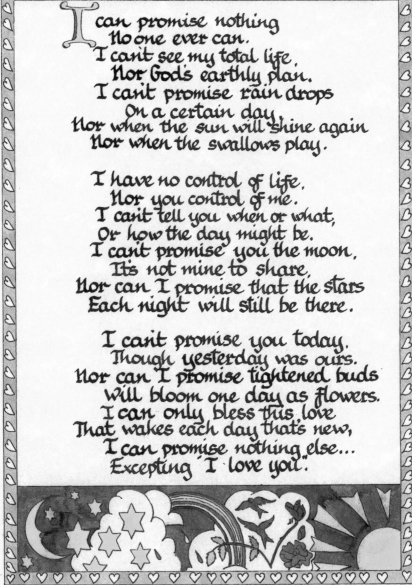

The Promise

I can promise nothing
   No one ever can.
I can't see my total life,
   Nor God's earthly plan.
I can't promise rain drops
   On a certain day,
Nor when the sun will shine again
Nor when the swallows play.

I have no control of life,
   Nor you control of me.
I can't tell you when or what,
Or how the day might be.
I can't promise you the moon,
   Its not mine to share,
Nor can I promise that the stars
Each night will still be there.

I can't promise you today,
   Though yesterday was ours.
Nor can I promise tightened buds
   Will bloom one day as flowers.
I can only bless this love
That wakes each day that's new,
   I can promise nothing else...
   Excepting I love you".

LYNN NEW ©

What Price?

What price love that chokes it's life with forceful care,
That binds it harsh between the vine
Protecting it with cherished looks and loving stare,
Yet hurts it so as lovers' hearts entwine?

?

What price this love that calls itself God-made & true
Yet suffocates with every step strayed from it's path
And all the love & longing this heart holds now for you
Will fade and die as embers on life's hearth?

?

What price this love whose fire raged so fierce,
Whose tender touch and hand brought flames to life?
Yet now possessive heart brings tears to pierce
And sudden words & silences cut as a surgeon's knife.

?

What price this love that cries it's blood in vain,
That knows each hill to climb is one from which to fall?
Who knows from giving much, has shared so much in gain
Yet, in the end, will we have shared at all?

?

What now, this love that's forced my heart to pay
A price so dear indeed, yet given full and free?
Let it pulse again with life indeed, I pray
Yet let my eyes be open; pained, though I must see.

?

What is this love that's brought us so to bear?
'Tis as a rose, picked, cherished and adored.
Better left to grow caressed by rain and air
A gentle love our hearts can well afford.

♥

The Human Factor

You can not be always wise
Nor say the right thing to appease.
You can not be always there
Or give of yourself just to please.
But to recognize weakness and strength
Will bring a balance anew,
Then you can acknowledge the truth
That you are in fact human too.

LYNN NEW ©

Guided Steps.

On virgin sands the footsteps that I tread
Show only now the life that I have led.
No sign in front to show the path I'll take,
Or those with greater courage I have yet to make.

Oh restless tide that turns incessantly
Wipe from me the pain and help me now to see
The footsteps that I planted were patterned by the past
Soon to be tide covered, I shall walk on at last.

The way that lies ahead upon the sea washed sand,
Yet now unmarked, soon will I understand,
The path not seen is marked upon the shore
By the hand that governs and the eye which sees far
more.

Reach Out

Why do you sound cold when I phone you,
  So distant and so far away?
  Could it be something you're feeling?
  My darling I wish you would say?
Tell me if we have a problem
  I'm empty and lonely inside.
  I feel that somehow I've failed you;
  The chasm between us lies wide.

Why are there times you won't mention
  The love that binds us so tight?
The calls that I make leave me wanting
It seems you have turned from my light.
  Is there a space in your longing?
  I'd fill it if only I could,
  But necessity bids we are parted,
Don't withdraw, but reach out as we should.

Can you not guess how I'm feeling?
  This parting is not of my choice,
It's something from which we both suffer
And I wait to be warmed by your voice;
But when it seems there's no effort
And the pauses are just empty space
  I feel that maybe I'll lose you
  Because we can't be in one place.

So when the cold light of morning
Does not warm when we speak on the phone,
Please try, oh please try to be thoughtful
  For in pain, you don't suffer alone.
Can't you see that when I'm not with you
  My life is like acting a part?
Don't distance yourself by withdrawal
  But comfort me now from your heart.

Tidal Turn

Nothing fills the aching void you leave,
  You must believe
    I love you still.
Nothing takes away the love of you
    For it is true
      I love you still.
Nothing tears and mends my heart, to learn
      Love's tidal turn
        I love you still.
Yet never now to show these words
Nor kiss and hold, hearts to enfold.
    Remember this, our parting kiss
        Tells you now
          I love you.

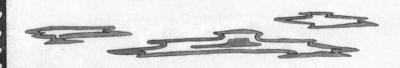

Blind Love

My love is blind, it cannot look or see
Nor can it touch, how can that be?
It cannot hold you in my arms nor squeeze you tight,
Nor kiss your lips a fond good night.

My love is blind, it cannot read your face,
Nor can my finger touch a smile to trace.
No body language can I read, mistakes to make,
Misguidedly I lie awake.

My love is blind, yet holds no sense of loss,
Though alone to turn and toss.
It cannot wake you with a sweet caress,
Nor finger touch away your stress.

My love is blind, fate forces us apart
Yet I see with beating heart
Though denied to us such precious time
God granted I am yours and you are mine.

love should be Understanding

Listen

Never do what I do,
Always what I tell you,
Do not step out bravely
Take a safer path.
Do not meet experience
As a form of growing
You'll be just as happy
Sitting by the hearth.

Why must you all tell me
"Things will soon get better"
If I hold on tightly
To a guarded rail?
Don't they know my heart cries
Not for mere existance,
But for arms to hold me,
Should I win or fail.

Words and strong opinions
Really count for nothing
Though I see they're offered
By caring folk and friends.
What they say I value
And will quietly listen
But I'll walk my own path
And turn the way it bends.

So when, at times, they tell me
What is best for my life,
What I ought to do
And where my future lies;
Help me Lord, to listen
Not to folk around me
But to your voice in my heart
It's strong, it's true, it's wise.

LYNN NEW ©

Flickering Flame

Are there only ashes
When love's fire dies,
When harsh words are spoken
And the spirit cries,
For all the things that once were
For all that might have been;
Never to be held again
Never to be seen?

Are there only embers
From love's dying Flame,
Never to be thought of
Except someone to blame?
All the loving moments
Pain and laughter shared
Blown to extinction
By the ones who cared.

Are there only klinkers
Where gentle hearts once bore
All the swift emotions
Yet beat in time no more?
Hard in pain and anguish
Bitter cold and black
I pray we can do better
Than blame each other's lack.

Watch the flame still smoulder
Though the embers pale.
It's not too late to kindle
Our love, with care, won't fail.
Time again to cherish
And with caring thought
Love will Fan the Flames
That we again have sought.

Heart's Harbour

At first there were no lights upon life's sea,
The boat I sailed was in fact me.
The wind blew and currents ran,
The ocean deep filled life's earthly span.
Once anchor weighed the journey had begun,
My compass guide were both the stars and sun.
From these my soul would learn to recognize
And slowly they'd become my comfort and my eyes.

Every now and then emotions did becalm,
A sense of peace ensued, subsiding my alarm.
The waves and growing storm would whip the sea,
I was fearful then of what life asked of me,
And yet my boat was safe and strong
Though the sea was often rough and journey long.
Oft I saw a shore line upon horizon clear
Despite the urgent longing, never to grow near.

Yet upon my journey I learned many things,
How to sail my own craft, how the spirit sings.
How to pray when life blows up a storm,
To give out thanks for calming seas and breezes warm,
How to tend the sails, taking in the slack,
Discovering my strength and the things I lack.
Finding courage, learning how to stand
When the boat is rocking and life gets out of hand.

Now I see a land mass forming fast
And feel that very soon I'll be home at last,
In a familiar harbour my spirit calls my home
Somewhere sure to moor my boat, safe from storm and foam.
So long upon life's seas I've fought my way
I find it hard to realise that I'm allowed to stay
Safe within the shelter my heart has cried to find;
Life's sea gave me my freedom and you my peace
of mind.

love should be

on-threatening

The Lion:The Lamb

Help me feed the lion
That lives inside of me.
That's born of spirit's longing
And creativity.
Help me feed the lion
And I will love the lamb
That dwells within your body
And makest you the man.
Your lamb does need great loving
That is mine to give;
My lion needs the courage
Learning how to live.
Let us, in our loving
Fill each other's need,
That the lion and the lamb
Together, both may feed.

LYNN NEW

'The Lily Pond'

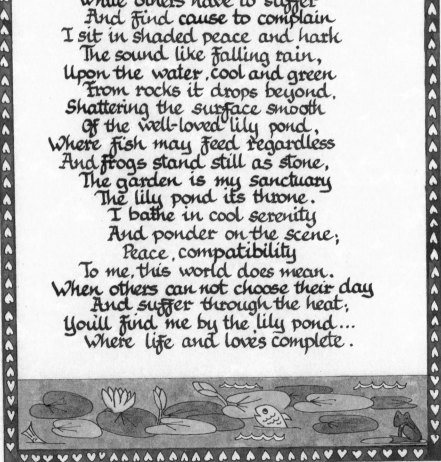

Oh, what bliss when heat seals
The Fate of you and I
When the golden sun does reign
Within the cloudless sky.
When men must rest, cloth-capped in shade
And women take the cool
Within their homes and work-place;
But me, I'm by the pool.
While others have to suffer
And find cause to complain
I sit in shaded peace and hark
The sound like falling rain,
Upon the water, cool and green
From rocks it drops beyond,
Shattering the surface smooth
Of the well-loved lily pond,
Where fish may feed regardless
And frogs stand still as stone,
The garden is my sanctuary
The lily pond its throne.
I bathe in cool serenity
And ponder on the scene;
Peace, compatibility
To me, this world does mean.
When others can not choose their day
And suffer through the heat;
You'll find me by the lily pond ...
Where life and love's complete.

love should be Expressive

Facets of Love

To those who know so little of love
I ask them to think again,
Does not your heart respond in part
To the sound of the soft Spring rain?

Are you not moved to some degree
By sunlight slanting through
The Autumn leaves of ancient trees?
Love won't let go of you.

And can't you see the incoming sea
Filling a translucent pool?
Like mist-filled eyes reflect the skies
Like some poor love-sick fool.

And do you not feel a shivering thrill
When kissed by a butterfly's wings?
Or a joy to the heart, an uplifting start
When a bird in the morning sings?

For those who know so little of love
Are only partially living.
Shut not the door on what love has in store
For nature's complete in her giving.

love should be Whole

Conclusion.

This prayer is raised for all who share
The common beating heart
Who know that love and life are one.
That each will play their part.
Yet when the lovers lose their day
When they sleep alone
Let them share again, Oh Lord
The Greatest Love they've known.